FIGS. 56–58.—A Thatched Barrel.

...ntal, and will ...eciated by your

...eep the English ...y, the bluebirds ...y sort of a shel-

buttonhole-stitch, and cord ...rose, the effect is charming.

NICKEL

...lye the sticks brown, and ...ve them an artistic purple. ...ke holes at the ends of our ...ng so we must be careful not

To make the holes, which ...we should use a gimlet, but ...e the holes without splitting ... use a red-hot wire for the ...rpose, heating it again when-...r it gets cool. The latter ...cess is slow and tedious, ...l we should not adopt it ...ess we are compelled to do

...Then we thread the wires ...ough the holes, as seen in the ...ture. The wires are twisted ...ether at the top ends, from ...ich our fern basket hangs. ... may, if we like, varnish the ...ket after we have made it. ...ross the bottom we should ... one or two cross sticks, so as ...o away with the wide open-

...Then we line the bottom ... all four sides with green ...ss, which we can procure for ...selves in the woods. Having ...ne so, we put a layer of stones ...ottom and fill up the basket ...in which we place the fern. ...ater the fern, we ought not ...n top of the basket. We ...vn and dip the entire basket ...t remain for half an hour. ...ter is best, but tap water ...ot easily get either of these.

Rustic Flower Vases

A simple and effective flower container for the summer cottage or porch is made from a short length of a tree branch. The bark gives a rustic appearance to the vase, and a variety of effects are obtainable by judicious selection, the white bark of the birch being the most conspicuous. The container may be made of any diameter by using a section of the desired size, from which the interior has been gouged or drilled out. A "liner," which is what florists call a container for water in such vases, may be provided by inserting a can, or other receptacle, into the hollow center.

If we can keep th sparrows away, the will nest in any sor tered hole.

Earthenware fl as shown in Fig. 5 used for bird-hous enlarge the holes bottoms to serve ways, and enclose

which when neatly ... bird friends.

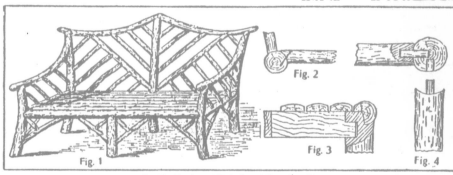

Rustic Seat and Details of Construction

How to Make a Rustic Seat

The rustic settee illustrated in Fig. 1 may be made 6 ft. long, which will accommodate four average-sized persons. It is not advisable to exceed this length, as then it would look out of proportion, says the Wood-Worker. Select the material for the posts, and for preference branches that are slightly curved, as shown in the sketch. The front posts are about 3½ in. in diameter by 2 ft. 4 in. long. The back posts are 3 ft. 4 in. high, while the center post is 3 ft. 8 in. in height. The longitudinal and transverse rails are about 3 in. in diameter and their ends are pared away to fit the post to which they are connected by 1-in. diameter dowels. This method is shown in Fig. 4. The dowel holes are bored at a distance of 1 ft. 2½ in. up from the lower ends of posts. The front center leg is partially halved

rails, and are then secured with two or three brads at each end.

Select curved pieces, about 2½ in. in diameter, for the arm rests and back rails; while the diagonally placed filling may be about 2 in. in diameter. Start with the shortest lengths, cutting them longer than required, as the paring necessary to fit them to the rails and posts shortens them a little. Brad them in posi... ...fitted, and try to ar... ...inter-vals.

A FER

FOR an expenditure o very little trouble, a make a pretty fern ba into the woods and colle about three-quarters o varying in length from inches. We shall re and forty pieces altoge

When we take these we must score down t from end to end of the and then, having put t a pail, we pour boiling on them. The effect scalding will be to strip bark, leaving us nothing bare sticks, which ar what we want for our p

Besides the sticks wh have collected, all the n we require is a little co brass wire, which we ca chase for five cents. Co brass wire is better th wire, because iron wire rust through and waste It will be seen that the tapers from about twelve square at the top to al at the bottom. Of cou to these sizes; we can inches at the bottom a top, or any other size th We may colour the s into water in which we h of permanganate of p

rustic country

Handmade Accents
for the Home

rustic country

Handmade

Accents for the Home

Abby Ruoff

Photography by Michael Watson

GIBBS·SMITH
P
PUBLISHER

SALT LAKE CITY

To my husband Carl and for our grandsons, Ben, Sam, and Adam.

First Edition
05 04 03 02 01 00   5 4 3 2 1

Text copyright © 2000 by Abby Ruoff
Photographs copyright © 2000 by Michael Watson
Photographs styled by Jim Williams and Abby Ruoff

Published by
Gibbs Smith, Publisher
P.O. Box 667
Layton, Utah 84041

Orders: (1-800) 748-5439
Web site: www.gibbs-smith.com

Edited by Suzanne Taylor
Designed and produced by Traci O'Very Covey
Printed and bound in Hong Kong

Library of Congress Cataloging-in-Publication Data

Ruoff, Abby.
    Rustic country: handmade accents for the home / Abby Ruoff; photographs by Michael Watson.
        p. cm.
    ISBN 0-87905-979-6
1. Nature craft. 2. Decoration and ornament, rustic. 3. House furnishings. I. Title.

TT857.R86 2000
745.5—dc21

00-029724

acknowledgments

A special thank you to my editor, Suzanne Taylor, for giving me the keys to the car so that I could explore new roads, and to photographer Michael Watson and stylist Jim Williams, both of whom helped me steer it.

Have little ornamental and useful things made by your own hands: they will indicate that
the dwelling has an animating and interested soul.

introduction

A note to
the reader

have you ever noticed that there are some rooms that seem to please the eye as much as the spirit? Whether it is a room you are seeing for the first time or the feeling that surrounds you when you recall a warm and cozy space from the past, these are the rooms we love to enter. Perhaps it is a vision recalled from a favorite book or movie or the memory of morning sunlight streaming in across a worn farmhouse kitchen floor. Real or imagined, these scenes are symbols of the essence of a true place of solitude and renewal. Some rooms have that lived-in quality, with mismatched secondhand sofas and chairs, hand-crocheted afghans, wood-paneled walls lined with books, and subtle-hued

The graceful twig candle stand, made from a multi-forked branch, is an enchanting handmade addition to this quiet corner where country furnishings set a restful scene.

A charming miniature chair serves as rustic sculpture in this master bedroom.

Some of your favorite things may be a little willow chair or a basket of pinecones: individual items that help to celebrate the joys of childhood and the pleasures of nature.

Oriental carpets. These are comfortable rooms. Then there are the interiors where great attention is given to details, bright airy spaces with contemporary sofas, crisp slipcovered chairs, and generous windows—well-edited rooms where the main ingredients are a few cherished objects and the mood is cool and calm. Each of these rooms has a welcoming elegance all its own that reflects personal style.

Personal style is the unexpected mix of elements that refuses to rely on clichés. It could be a twig wall sconce hanging amidst gilt-framed Victorian oil paintings or a multi-forked twig used as a key caddie on a cabin wall. Or it might be as elaborate as scalloped birch-bark-trimmed shelves in a country corner cupboard housing a collection of grandmother's china or as ordinary as a split birch limb used for bookends. Some

An eclectic blend of furnishings mixes happily in this rustic-country bedroom where antique linen sheets are used as curtains. The vintage calico quilt that tops the bed is paired with new toile fabric for a dust ruffle. On the bedside table are examples of family treasures, a Victorian book of poetry, a teapot for one, and an antique Danish telephone.

of your favorite things may be a little willow chair or a basket of pinecones: individual items that help to celebrate the joys of childhood and the pleasures of nature. These are the basics that never go out of fashion and prove that rooms needn't be elaborate to communicate hospitality. Livable rooms can be found anywhere, and their inspiration is everywhere. Whether one prefers a penthouse apartment on Manhattan's trendy upper West Side or a rambling ranch house in the middle of Utah, a halcyon welcome awaits those who enter these special spaces.

Which brings us to the question: What is that elusive quality that invites us in? To me, it's probably what the ancient Roman writer Martial called *Rus un urbe*, "country in the town"— loosely translated as bringing a bit of nature indoors. Like accessories in a wardrobe that are used to flatter a garment, a bouquet of autumn ferns, a bark basket, or a handmade twig lamp help enhance any room setting. It seems apparent now that throughout history, the human spirit has had an emotional need for balance. We can easily trace the first great rustic revival back to the

LEFT A rustic seat provides a natural element in this turn-of-the-century studio portrait of a young man.

RIGHT Allentown, Pennsylvania, November 1912. This young lady in her smart new hat poses with a rustic garden settee, as did many urban-dwellers of the day.

mid-nineteenth century, when city dwellers believed they required contact with nature to lead healthy moral lives. It was during this period that private and public gardens were sprouting seats of twisted, gnarled laurel and rhododendron, and Reverend Murray was touting the virtues of nature. In 1869 William H. Murray, pastor of Boston's Park Street Church, published *Adventures in the Wilderness or Camp-Life in the Adirondacks*. His premise was that "man" cannot escape the need for nature, for the woods "to have a chance to think and feel. . . . The religion of the forest," he told his supporters, "is emotional and poetic." City dwellers were encased in the excesses of civilization, and Murray (along with other visionaries of the time) attempted to inspire visitors, campers, and fishers to the Adirondack

wilderness. When the great adventure failed in the summer of 1869 (due to cold wet weather along with pesky mosquitoes and black flies), visitors and sportsmen were more than satisfied to bring back a bit of rusticity for their townhouses—*Rus un urbe*. Chairs, tables, and plant stands were finding their way home, and soon many a New York City apartment sprouted furnishings from the woods of the great North Country. In spite of Murray's failure to convert a party of partisans to join him on his two- or three-month stays in the wilderness, word spread and the aura of the forest primeval appealed to wealthy urbanites.

During the last half of the nineteenth century, many of the rich and famous—including the Rockefellers, Morgans, and Vanderbilts—had rustic "camps" built and enjoyed summer solitude in

Interiors were fashioned of exposed wood, log beams, and naturally formed twig railings.

Rustic furniture made
of cedar, white birch,
yellow birch, hickory,
laurel, and willow
furnished entire rooms.

Catskill Mts.

these mansions. Interiors were fashioned of exposed wood, log beams, and naturally formed twig railings. Rustic furniture made of cedar, white birch, yellow birch, hickory, laurel, and willow furnished entire rooms. Natural decorative elements such as bark, burl, moss, pinecones, and fan-shaped fungus formations were often used to complete these one-of-a-kind pieces. From the hot-springs resorts of Alabama, Kentucky, and Virginia to the mountain retreats of the Adirondacks, the Catskills, and the Great Smokies, the back-to-nature movement gained momentum and a new industry was created—tourism. The artificial conditions of city life that were created during the beginning of the Industrial Revolution helped to carry the ideas of such notables as editor

William Cullen Bryant and naturalist John Burroughs to the newly formed middle class. And it was this middle class that made up the growing group of tourists, first traveling by stagecoach line and steamboat and later by train. Eventually the effect of the automobile at the beginning of the twentieth century had the greatest impact on the tourist industry, and roadside hotels, campsites, and eateries sprang up along new state highways. Mountain craftspeople found a ready market in selling rustic work to the hordes of tourists who soon became commonplace during the warm summer months. Some of the finest surviving examples of antique pieces of twig and bark furnishings were created during this period.

Given the warmth and quirky charm

Given the warmth and quirky charm that rustic elements can add to a home, it's no surprise that renewed interest in these handmade accents has surfaced now as we enter this high-tech century.

929:—SQUIRREL INN, HAINES FALLS, CATSKILL MTS., N. Y.

Large-letter postcards helped advertise rustic vacation spots to the folks back home, encouraging tourism.

that rustic elements can add to a home, it's no surprise that renewed interest in these handmade accents has surfaced now as we enter this high-tech century. It seems only natural that we realize the need for a counterbalance to the wave of intimidating electronic gadgets and gizmos flooding our rooms and overflowing our houses. What it comes down to is that the human spirit has not really changed that much, and we still have an emotional need for balance; it is by bringing the outdoors in, by con-

necting to nature, that our homes become our anchor.

What a great way to begin anew: tap into the information age, resolve to develop your taste, create personal space, celebrate your heritage, connect to nature, bring the outdoors in, and include a bit of creativity in your home so that your rooms please the eye as much as the senses.

Welcome to
RUSTIC COUNTRY!

greetings from rustic country

Just a note
to make you
feel happy

after a long journey with trends, fads, and places that had "the look," we arrived here, back home, where rooms are not serious, but are expressive. Something about the place awakened memories that I never knew I had, or at least had forgotten about. I see it now; outside, the grass in the front yard is kept mowed. I think I can still close my eyes and smell the damp, sweet fragrance of the soft green clippings of clover and ryegrass, as the well-oiled push mower slices them up. The backyard is never mowed, and through every season we rediscover our own flower meadow. Here, the wildflowers jump and sprout to our delight. First come the paintbrushes, red and yellow, dainty blue-eyed

A sunny October afternoon provides the perfect opportunity for enjoying a picnic just before putting the raft ashore for the winter.

grass, silver-tipped yarrow, wild phlox, and low-growing huckleberry shrubs. Mid- and late summer bring a riot of color with daisies and black-eyed Susans dotting the tall field of red-top grass. Pale purple Joe Pye weed and bright white Queen Anne's lace gently dance in the late summer breeze near the ancient red barn and silver gray woodshed. And every year, autumn arrives with the impressive beauty of the gold-

enrod, pinkish-purple New England asters, and wild blue chickory. We are connected to nature here by color.

On the south side of the house, the clothesline is strung up between the two stately sugar maples. When the heavy wet laundry causes the line to sag, it is propped up with a sturdy forked branch. All of today's commercial "fresh-air" fabric softeners and dryer sheets combined cannot even hope to

A hillside path, out behind the barn where the old horse rake rests.

20

A forked branch helps to keep a sagging clothesline taut out here in rustic country, where the clothes smell cleaner when they are dried outside.

One whiff of freshly laundered bedding and you cannot wait to hop into bed.

come close to duplicating the original scent of line-dried laundry. One whiff of freshly laundered bedding and you cannot wait to hop into bed. You are suddenly ten years old again. Behind the starched white linen curtains, the night sky is crisp and clear with a riot of stars dotting the heavens. We are connected to nature here by fragrance.

Best of all, this place has reawakened the child in all of us and allowed us to create. Can you remember using logs for chairs and benches, along with acorn cups for the dolls' tea party? I see the children now, down by the stream, setting up the velvet-moss flat rock to make a "store," with pebbles for coins and wild mint and watercress for produce. They are resourceful, just like the grown-ups. They see their mother cover a farm table with red-and-white-checked oilcloth, their father fashion a

The romance of a bygone era and relaxed lifestyle is displayed here, where forked willow twigs and a seat of salvaged barn wood create a backyard swing.

Can you remember using logs for chairs and benches, along with acorn cups for the dolls' tea party?

A little mountain stream reads the stepping-stones as words and hears the water as a song.

swing out of supple willow twigs. It seems everyone is making something out of nothing and enjoying it. Suddenly we are children again, trusting our instincts, being creative, resourceful, and inventive. "Don't worry about whether it will please your neighbor, although that is very nice," warned folk artist Peter Hunt, "but be sure to please yourself." We are connected to nature here by memory.

This place is one thing, and yet it is everything. On the way here we thought of lines from T. S. Eliot: "Be remembered; invoked with past and future. Only through time time is conquered . . . time before and time after." Here, it is as much a state of mind as it is a "style." It's a beach house on the rocky coast of Maine, a mountain chalet along the ridge of a Colorado ski slope, a farmhouse on the Kansas prairie, a

lakeside cabin, a suburban ranch house, a retirement home.

Best of all, it's you. It is as individual and special as the folks who live here.

Down the road there is a little stone house of but three rooms, all graced with rustic elegance. Valuable oil paintings rest on twig easels, and pinecones sit in sterling silver sugar bowls.

Way across town there is the most charming little log cabin in the woods, where all manner of kitsch and collectibles delight the eye. One of the joys of this area is discovering the variety and yet the sameness every time I walk through a door.

Out where corduroy fields dot the landscape stands a clapboard farmhouse, generations old. Colorful quilts grace the beds, and handmade baskets are used for everything from portable cradles to laundry totes as well as picking berries.

But for all their differences, these places share certain similarities: they are all part and parcel of homes called *Rustic Country*.

By bringing the outdoors in, we connect to nature here. It's honest and it's true, and by letting rustic in we find that it is possible to have a personal place with balance and style.

You just can't get this feeling out on

We stopped along our walk to see the birds gather together for their long southern flight.

"OVERLOOK" SILVER BAY ASSOCIATION ON LAKE GEORGE, N. Y.

By bringing the outdoors in, we connect to nature here.

the highway at the super-saver store. Woodland treasures and handmade objects are as much a part of rustic-country rooms as are windows that let the sunlight in and doors that welcome friends.

While the look here is "country," one cannot fully discern its heritage. Flowered chintz spells English country, while calico and homespun fabrics represent American country. So much is made available to us today that many here find it easy to duplicate the nostalgia and history of French, Italian, or Swedish country. What they all have in common, however, is a respect for what has gone before, new-world imagination, easy elegance, and plain old-fashioned ingenuity. I'm finding this to

be a neighborly atmosphere where your dreams, waking or sleeping, influence your world.

What strikes me is now that I'm here, I arrived basically where I started—back home! This place has jarred my memory, and I find myself seeing familiar things for the first time again. In order for you to get here, you will have to drive yourself and find your own way, but I'm sending you some pictures as a guide.

Having a wonderful time! Wish you were here!

Yours from the country, waiting for the first frost,

A.R.

Look no further for the anatomy of rustic country.

The sugarhouse is quiet now, the evaporator sold, but the monument still stands.

Crafted generations ago,
the old weathered shed
door is still in use.

Grandfather's cherished hand-crafted rustic ladder remains reliable. We see it now as a tribute to the creative spirit that is our heritage.

A child's dress turned into a clothespin bag is a playful addition to the country clothesline.

For us who are true to the trail:

A vision to seek, a beckoning peak,

A farness that never will fail.

—Robert W. Service, *Rhymes of a Rolling Stone*

autumn

A time
to gather

Although there is no single season that best reflects rusticity, if I had to choose one it would be autumn—late autumn, when a carnival of color cuts loose and spreads its carpet on the forest floor. The October woods are remarkable in that when so much appears to be decaying, we can detect a new beginning if we take the time to look and listen. We can hear the wedge of wild geese overhead as they honk through the purple sky. A peek under moist, rich pine needles can lead to the delicate beauty of late-growing lacy ferns or intriguing toadstools. It is now that the striped chipmunks and gray squirrels scurry about gathering nuts and seedpods for their winter root cellars.

A stroke of brilliant color washes our world.

Our stately maple tree is the first to turn colors and its leaves are the first to fall.

For those who rely on nature's bounty for household accents and furnishings, autumn is the best time to look to the forest and actually see the trees.

I remember reading once that the Native Americans referred to October as "the leaf-falling moon"; I, however, prefer to think of it as "the gathering moon." Along with the showy leaf colors, golden ferns, and spirited rose hips, a bountiful harvest is one of autumn's most memorable scenes. Although most of us don't live on, or even nearby, farms any longer, October has the power to remind us of busy hands collecting fruits from field, vineyard, and orchard. It is a time of country-crisp air and sunny days, when pumpkins are in their prime and an apple has a mouth-cleansing tang it will never have again.

For those who rely on nature's bounty for household accents and furnishings, autumn is the best time to look to the forest and actually see the trees.

Say hello to a
bright afternoon
when pumpkins
and pears, tasty
harbingers of
autumn, set
the scene, and
sunbeams signal an
impromptu rest.

Suddenly the woods are open and full of surprise. The bare tree skeletons inspire our designs and help discover new ways of experiencing creativity. Sometimes what we see in the woods opens up new possibilities, such as the diameter and shape of a forked limb or the length of a knobby branch. I'm always on the look-out for these interesting configurations to form comfortable chair backs or practical shelf supports. Whether it's the feel of a smooth young sapling or the texture of aged bark, nature's gifts are just waiting to come home with us.

Try walking the woodland trails at different times of the day, and each time you return you will begin to notice something new. Some of my favorite "finds" include turning up a freshly shed deer antler at twilight and spotting a

A wreath of grapevine trims the collar of a tin sap bucket filled with the last ferns of summer.

When placed inside, these bouquets provide a link to the out-of-doors and deliver a heaping dose of casual elegance.

bunch of fallen hemlock boughs adorned with a multitude of dainty pinecones after an early morning rainstorm. Soon you will find yourself looking at things through the eyes of an artist. Many of the somewhat ordinary elements, such as fragments of moss-covered logs and irregular-shaped stones, make elegant compositions when grouped together indoors. The forest floor is truly paved with treasures, and everything from acorns to birch-bark curls can yield prizes to enhance the rustic integrity of your dwelling.

While the woods and forests that surround my house are inspirational, a

Happy is the day when we see the grandeur of autumn on the bank and the pond.

stroll along a country road can be just as compelling. Many a familiar route takes on a completely new appearance when one walks instead of driving by at forty or fifty miles an hour. I'm sure you know the feeling; you can whiz right past the sumac tree with flaming spikes, determined to get someplace fast while not even seeing the obvious. While you are taking your autumn walk, you may notice, here and there, the papaw shrubs that show red berries now, or the burning bush that paints the landscape scarlet. If you happen on a witch-hazel thicket, you will be surprised to discover that it is now, in late October, when the witch hazel begins to bloom and brighten the underbrush with yellow fringy petals. Along the way you will probably want to gather some of the recently fallen boughs of red oak and sugar maple to help decorate your house. When placed inside,

Harvested birch poles, waiting to be turned into furnishings, lean on a venerable old shed in the dappled sunlight.

Shadows fall across the peaceful stack of ancient limbs.

these bouquets provide a link to the out-of-doors and deliver a heaping dose of casual elegance.

When gathering materials, don't neglect some of the sturdy roadside vines such as Virginia creeper, wood vine, wild grapevine, honeysuckle, and even pesky kudzu. Wild blackberry and raspberry vines are useful for a variety of projects, but they must be dethorned. Wear heavy gloves when working with

thorny vines or rose-hip branches. Vines without their fancy summer dress allow us to find their wispy limbs, and these supple climbers can be put to good use for a variety of weaving and wrapping projects. Wild grapevine seems to grow in profusion around my part of the country. With sprouting curlicues, their runners look like nature's whimsy, and yet their length and strength are perfect for weaving serviceable baskets and decorative

A work in progress. We are thankful for warm days to continue our projects outside, for it won't be long before we will have to close our doors and work inside. This sconce will come in handy for the approaching longer nights.

wreaths. Keep your eye out for highway crews trimming roadside overgrowth; this stuff is usually headed for the chipper, and in some towns you are encouraged to cart it away.

For city dwellers, a ramble through the park can provide a wealth of fascinating materials if you set out intent upon discovery. Even the smallest park may provide a better place than you suspect to gather twigs and limbs. Pristine trees and shrubs are constantly being trimmed in order to maintain their "civilized" shape and control their growth. These pruned parts can be gathered into fanciful clusters to grace a

Here stands our old friend with memories of childhood play beneath its sturdy branches.

GREETINGS FROM THE ADIRONDACK MTS., N. Y.   4A-H1569

dining table or window ledge. A simple collection of acorns, pinecones, and autumn leaves can be a natural alternative to a traditional centerpiece. Go to the same park often and become familiar with the paths. You may not see much at the onset, but each step will introduce you to something new. When you get to know every brick, every bench, every bend along the paths, your eyes will open, and with a little bit of imagination your city place will have the rustic-country touch.

Harvesting and
Cutting the Wood

Autumn days are just perfect for harvesting wood for winter projects. While it's true that early rustic builders advocated cutting trees in the winter when the sap was down, following the theory that winter cutting will preserve the bark, I find the warm, fall days more enjoyable and have built many projects from autumn-cut wood. Because rustic work is not an exact science, it is a good idea to cut a few more limbs than you think you will need. Once the wood gets home, some of the branches will inspire creations other than what you first saw in the woods. It's also comforting to have a stockpile set aside, but if you are a beginner, don't get carried away with the cutting—remember, you have to keep it dry once you get it home. A warm winter basement and heated garage are excellent locations if you are fortunate to have such sites. If you have

Once the wood gets home, some of the branches will inspire creations other than what you first saw in the woods.

Muted colors of stone and wood claim their place in the sun.

to store it outdoors, it is a good idea to turn it and check it for unwanted critters from time to time.

Most wood eaters feed on dead trees in warm weather, so wood stored outside in cold weather is not usually a target. If your wood supply has to be kept outdoors for a prolonged period, however, pay careful attention to any tiny holes or deep channels that appear on the logs. This is not always a sure-fire method for detecting insect activity, but it is a clue

for further investigation. If you find small piles of sawdust around or near the holes, the limb should be discarded.

If signs of insect activity appear on a completed project, you will have to spray with an insecticide. Several safe, effective insecticides are available. Check with your local nursery or hardware store, and make sure the product you choose is safe for indoor use. While you should use a product that is made with a natural botanical pyrethrin base,

With a nod to nature's artwork, the display is perfect: the elements are ordered by placement, shape, and tone. Vibrant leaves punctuate the textured, mossy green stone, creating a masterpiece.

depending on the percentage of pyrethrins it contains, it may be inappropriate for inside use. All insecticides should be applied outdoors.

Cut the wood with care using sharp tools (axes, saws, or clippers). Never rip or tear the branches, as this can destroy a living plant. If you plan to make small pieces, or nailed joinery, drying the wood in advance is not necessary. If you are working with willow, you want it to be fresh (green) so that it is pliable. When cutting willow, leave more than you remove so that you are assured a

plentiful future supply. Willow's strength and flexibility is invaluable for making many projects. Willow shoots usually remain flexible for up to two weeks after harvesting, but it is a good idea to soak the autumn shoots in a bucket of water in a cool place until you are ready to use them. Permit yourself a few practice tries at bending and arching the willow before you begin your final project. With a little practice, the novice can soon become an expert. Slow and steady is the secret to successful willow bending.

Nothing says
country like a
group of walking
sticks, and this
trio reflects
rustic-country
romance.

Warmed by a ray of morning sunlight, a seasonal display graces the barn door.

October clouds
circulate at dawn and the
lake is covered with
early morning mist.

The view from this rustic-
country front porch
overlooks a portion of
the lake with Majestic
Mountain in the distance.

Sunrise light on
the shore paints
our world with
vibrant colors to
welcome the day.

Lost in time—the country scene is set.

The focus of this
moment comes
each year, and yet
we are surprised to
see it here.

Fallen trees provided the legs for this rustic stool; its seat, found at a flea market, will be attached this winter.

rustic elegant style

The sophisticated side of rustic
comes home to upscale,
but keeps its down-home appeal.

"rustic" and "elegant" may sound incompatible, but in reality nothing charms the eye like the graceful balance achieved with these interacting elements. Balance is the stabilizing force that establishes good design and brings order out of chaos, sheltering us while welcoming us home. Textural balance helps individualize our homes and create pleasing environments. We are comfortable here; it's the place of strong rugged chairs and soft downy cushions. We see our grandmother's silver candlesticks on top of the primitive jelly cupboard. We remember fancy lace curtains on the rustic farmhouse door. And we can feel the gracious hospitality at the neighbor's table when she serves

Creating a new use for an old favorite. A rustic plant stand serves up some bubbly for a special occasion.

lemonade and cookies from cut glass and crystal in her rustic twig gazebo. When we discover how to bridge the gap between the woods and the town—while making the best of both—we create the look of rustic elegance.

This pas de deux with nature creates a new look for a new century and adds gentle elegance, equally as comfortable with silver and damask or bark and twigs. Here we have it—the refined shine of an heirloom tea set, the vintage charm of velvet cushions combined with rusticated home furnishings—the sophisticated mix that establishes individuality. To keep rooms alive and interesting and

make a home sparkle with verve, add a measure of the unexpected. It is this imaginative dash that actually pulls objects together, creating an informal setting with formal overtones—one that's elegant yet comfortable.

elements
of style

Walls

Paint is the most common and least expensive way to cover walls. With the great variety of paints now available, anyone can learn a variety of techniques

Rich in personal character, this bedroom combines myriad country styles, including a pair of brass twin beds joined to create king-sized comfort. An empire settee, at the foot of the bed, and a nearby pine blanket chest further enhance the rustic-country feeling. Next to the bed, a schoolmaster's desk and a treasured Old Hickory arm-chair complete the room.

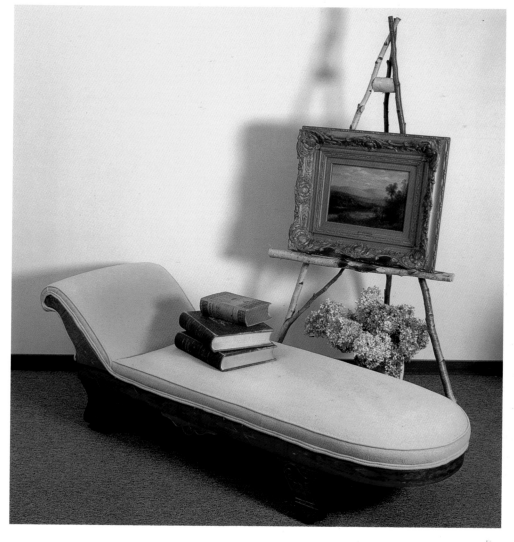

Classic simple beauty really shows here with a very personal mix of furnishings. A Hudson River oil painting on a twig easel is grouped near an Eastlake recamier, bringing home substance and style. This easel can be made by adjusting the scale and following the directions for the tabletop easel.

When we discover how to bridge the gap between the woods and the town—while making the best of both—we create the look of rustic elegance.

to turn plain walls into fantasy finishes. For easy elegance, use a natural sea sponge to dab or rub on a glaze made from water-diluted paint. For a sophisticated effect, use various shades of white on a white wall. The subtle result will astound you and coat even the most humdrum wall with energy. Divide a wall with a chair rail, either real or painted. Paint the bottom half of the wall with a solid color or a faux wood grain. Paint the top half in a contrasting color or, for a softer effect, sponge on a gold or silver glaze using water-based acrylic paints. A particularly elegant background may be achieved by covering walls with fabric. The soft texture of natural linen imparts an easy elegance in rustic spaces.

Floors

Add interest to new or worn floors with paint or stain. If painting floors in high traffic areas, it is a good idea to use a protective topcoat. Polyurethane varnish is an oil-based product; it's hard wearing and takes about six to ten hours to dry. It comes in flat, satin, and

A twig plant holder takes on a new role when antique hurricane shades replace clay flowerpots. Tiny tea lights are lit just before the first guests arrive for a festive event, and the front door beckons with rustic charm.

high-gloss finishes, clear or stained. If using clear, choose a non-yellowing variety. Acrylic varnish is water-based, does not yellow, and dries in one to two hours. It is not as hard wearing, so you will want to use several coats.

Area Rugs

Painted or polished floors benefit from the warm and subtle colors of a handmade vintage Oriental rug. At estate sales, be on the lookout for wonderful aged rugs. If the rug is worn, all the better, for that's part of the charm of old textiles. Avoid holes or stains, for it is usually too costly to have holes repaired and old stains are rarely removable. If the price is right, however, consider a tattered rug if there are some salvageable areas that can be turned into pillows.

Windows

Drapery poles can be crafted of natural twigs and branches. For unexpected drama, paint these the color of metal to convey a gentle atmosphere. Use natural pinecones for finials or tiebacks to embellish curtains. Lengthen curtains or trim valances with pinecone or acorn trims. Make your own woodland window toppers: Cut a triangular pediment out of plywood. Using a glue gun or epoxy glue, attach an assortment of woodland treasures such as bark pieces, leaves, moss, and pinecones. Hang it like a painting on top of the window. A wood valance can be fashioned in the same manner.

Details

Fabrics

While many new fabrics are perfectly at home in rustic settings, faded vintage textiles blend with the scheme and set the mood. Natural linen and cotton, along with inexpensive muslin, are three good choices for drapes, curtains, and

Drapery poles can be crafted of natural twigs and branches.

RIGHT An elegant rustic swag of bent grapevine—flecked with gold leaf and draped with a silk chiffon scarf—tops this antique mirror in a country house. A gold-painted twig platform holds a bouquet of roadside clippings.

shades. Velvet, old or new, imparts luxury and helps soften a room. Fabric can be instantly aged with a tea bath or fabric dye. To age fabric with tea, mix up a brew (the stronger the tea, the darker the color) and immerse the wet cloth to create the desired tint. Practice with scraps before the final dip. Color dyes are sold in supermarkets and discount stores in powdered and liquid forms in almost every imaginable color. Follow the directions on the package for turning textiles your color of choice. Old velvet usually takes dye very well, but when using new velvet, choose the all-cotton variety.

Accessories

Walls

Adding mirrors to rustic frames is one of the best ways there is to grace your walls. Not only do mirrors reflect light and add a feeling of space to a small room, but they also reflect the furnishings. While finding rustic frames may not be easy, making your own is rather simple when you start with a purchased frame,

Silver treasures mix with cones and sickle pears to transform a proud old farmhouse scene into an elegant setting.

Off the wall onto the table. "There Is No Place Like Home" sets the scene at this luncheon table where ribbon-tied napkins are served in a Native American yarn basket and doll cradle. The craft-store wreath of winter wheat that encircles the antique ironstone bowl is another nod to new ways of using familiar items.

For simple bouquets of rustic elegance, nothing quite surpasses the graceful charm of modest branches.

either new or of the tag-sale variety. Use wood glue or a glue gun to adhere bark, twigs, moss, or pinecones (or a combination of these) to the existing frame.

Tabletops

Adding the glow of candles to a table makes a dramatic and elegant statement. Try making your own rustic candlestick with any hardwood branch. Make sure the branch stands firmly upright. Measure and mark the center top of the branch. Using a drill and the correct-sized bit, drill a hole approximately one inch deep at the center of the branch. For elegant outdoor dining, place these natural candleholders on tin trays and position glass hurricane shades over them. Note: Never leave burning candles unattended.

For simple bouquets of rustic elegance, nothing quite surpasses the graceful charm of modest branches. Flowering forsythia, quince, myrtle, and dogwood in spring; bright-red rose hips and the winding limbs of wild grapevine and Virginia creeper in the fall. For winter charm, bare branches weave their magic when the garden urns are brought inside and filled with birch limbs or gnarled apple boughs that happen to break off during a storm. Seemingly ordinary, these are valuable accessories that help make your environment rustic elegant.

birch ornaments

Materials

Selection of birch-log slices, 1 to 4 inches long

Reed or cane (usually used for basket making)

Step One

Drill a ½-inch-diameter hole through the length of each log slice.

Step Two

Soak the reed in a bucket of warm water to make it supple and cut it into pieces 6 to 8 inches long.

Step Three

Insert one end of the flexible reed in the log hole; form a loop and insert the remaining end. TIP: These delightful little ornaments make a handsome display hanging on bare branches as well as evergreens.

Out here, every season is cause for decorating.

Anticipating winter, our little spruce tree gets all dressed up.

place-card holder

Step One
Cut 1½-inch-diameter birch branches into 3-inch lengths.

Step Two
Use a circular saw to cut the logs in half and to cut a slit ½-inch deep.

A sprig of fresh rosemary tucked into birch-bark napkin rings perfumes the vintage damask napkins and helps create the perfect mood for an elegant rustic-country dinner party. Gold-rimmed plates, heirloom-silver flatware—along with birch-bark place-card holders and mini candlesticks—complete the setting on the vintage floral spread.

The summer fireplace, complete with white birch logs.

M'lady's chamber.

A natural-shaped rock, discovered on an autumn walk in the woods, provides a repository for jewelry on this
dresser, while a simple twig becomes a ring holder.

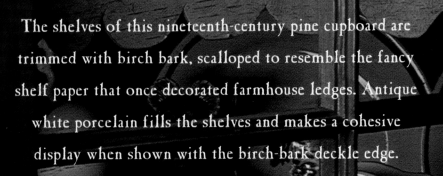

scallop trim

Materials

Sheets of pressed
birch bark
Scissors
Tacky adhesive or
double-sided tape

Instructions

Following the pattern
on the contents page,
cut the bark shapes
with sharp scissors or
create your own natural
shelf liner. Attach
to shelf with tacky
adhesive or double-
sided tape.

The shelves of this nineteenth-century pine cupboard are
trimmed with birch bark, scalloped to resemble the fancy
shelf paper that once decorated farmhouse ledges. Antique
white porcelain fills the shelves and makes a cohesive
display when shown with the birch-bark deckle edge.

A close-up of a rustic bedside desk shows a bark-covered book caddy and willow-wreath picture frame.

The handcrafted
stool, upholstered
in a vintage
coverlet remnant,
helps to make this
master bedroom
memorable.

A humble table, created out of scraps of wood from a box and four white birch legs, takes on a new importance when placed in front of an elegant Adams sofa upholstered in antique silk velvet. The juxtaposition of the satin souvenir pillows adds a lighthearted note.

twig sconce

Materials

Purchased twig sconce (available at most craft stores or garden centers)

Lamp-making electrical kit (available at most hardware stores and home centers)

Clip-on shade adapter (available at lighting centers or electrical supply stores)

Scraps of bark

2 brass paper fasteners

Heavy-duty sewing thread and needle

Low-wattage bulb (10-25 watts)

Step One

Install the electrical components, as pictured, according to the directions on the purchased kit.

Step Two

Arrange a folded piece of bark in the pocket of the sconce, masking the electrical components.

Step Three

For the shade, fold the bark into a cone shape. Adjust the size to suit the sconce. Hold the shade steady with one hand while securing it with the brass fasteners, along the back, through the two pieces of bark.

Step Four

Arrange the shade over the clip-on wire-shade adapter. Using heavy-duty thread and a sharp needle, stitch the cone shape to the wire adapter in several places.

Safety Tip:

Never leave the light on unattended.

Glistening light reflects from the gilt picture frames in this elegant country setting where a craft-store twig sconce is easily transformed into an electric light. The easy-to-follow project directions will inspire you to put your personal stamp on various purchased items.

Birches.

Birch bark can be photocopied
and used to make book covers.

Outdoors or indoors, any country setting can be turned into a gala event with this amusing candelabra.

Creative re-use. Although intended to hold flowerpots, this twig tray is cleverly used now as a hostess tray to serve drinks.

A tabletop arrangement reveals this gentleman's
delight in the elegant rustic-country style.
The hat stand is fashioned out of two naturally
forked branches.

twig hat stand

Step One

Locate a sturdy forked
branch for the base,
approximately 12 inches
long and 1 1/2 to 2 inches
in diameter. The center
post is a multi-forked
branch, 13 inches tall
and 1 inch in diameter.
You will also need a
round piece of 3/4-inch
wood, 7 inches in
diameter, for the top.

Step Two

The center post is
attached to the base
through the bottom
using a 3-inch spike.
Use a drill and a
1/4-inch wood-boring
bit to accommodate
the spike.

Step Three

Attach the wood top
piece, from the top,
with 1 1/2-inch finishing
nails.

A twig stand, dressed up in vintage green velvet and an edging
of Victorian trim rescued from a rummage sale.

A farmhouse wall,
lovingly hand
scraped and
reclaimed, not only
unveils layers of
paint but helps
record the history
for our children.

A piece of stamped bark helps anchor this tabletop still life. To make your own stamped bark, work on the inside of the bark. Use rubber stamps from the craft store (or make your own out of anything handy, such as a potato or a rubber eraser). Use acrylic craft paints in natural shades of brown and green to stamp your designs.

Not a grand bouquet but a handful of late summer's finery to remind us of another kitchen somewhere in the rustic country of our childhood.

rustic farmhouse style

Say hello to rustic farmhouse style,
where handmade is more common than store-bought
and down-to-earth can mean gardening.

Natural birch squares, tacked in place, provide a charming rustic game table for an afternoon of checkers. Among the many cherished items seen here are the flags and flag-related items, such as the cigar-felt appliquéd pillows.

rustic farmhouse style is rooted in our rural history, learning from and respecting the past. This regard, though we may choose to modify it, helps make our surroundings meaningful. The human touch is evident here, where personal attachments mix with contemporary possessions while the world outside shifts and turns like a northeast wind. Echoes of heritage resonate in these rooms where style and personality merge, where simple things mix readily with family treasures, and uncomplicated decorating draws you in. These spaces look unplanned, even if months were spent arranging, rearranging, and designing.

To achieve the casual farmhouse look, think of a story. Dip into early

recollections and imagine a setting where the younger generation moves into the family homestead, combining their possessions with inherited handcrafted items. These belongings, some fresh and current, some weathered and well used, become the inspiration for the story line and help spin the yarn.

Rustic farmhouse style is friendly—pure and simple. It's the sort of place where you are immediately at home, even though you have never been there before. The first thing that comes to mind is the kitchen. It is warm and welcoming, the busiest room in the house, with a well-used table and secondhand chairs, freestanding beadboard cabinets and open shelving, a large white porcelain sink and a six-burner stove, a whistling tea kettle, bean pots, and assorted baskets heaped with fresh vegetables. It's where friends gather for favorite foods, conversation, and good stories; it's where the "rustic" in farmhouse is interpreted with possessions borrowed from nature.

The quintessential rustic-country bedroom, complete with a painted iron bedstead, a handmade Boston Commons quilt, a cottage chest of drawers, a twig-trimmed oil painting, a rustic coat rack, and a twig stand.

A winsome whirligig—
mounted over the
entrance—is a symbol of
country charm.

Rustic farmhouse

style is friendly—

pure and simple.

Elements of Style

Walls

If you like the natural autumn colors—
terra-cottas, golds, flaming sumac, and
oak brown—use small doses to add
punch and verve to selected areas.
When thinking of color, white is always
right, from the soft look of oatmeal and
putty to shades of cafe au lait to a sprin-
kling of dove gray. Mix white walls
with green woodwork for a look that is
more "farm" than the usual country
blue and white. Use clear sunlit yellow
for a cheery kitchen, or try pale blue for
the ceiling on a memory-making porch.

Floors

While the soft honey glow of random-
width, wide-board pine may seem like
the floor of choice, there are any number
of options equally suitable for a rustic
farmhouse. Floors of brick, stone, or
clay tile have all the qualities of natural
beauty that enhance any setting. To
impart a subtle worn look to your wood
floor, try a color stain; for impact, use
opaque paint in any natural color.

Area Rugs

Color and pattern are handsomely
exhibited on rustic farmhouse floors
with small rugs, many of which are
handcrafted and familiar, such as the
hooked, braided, crocheted, or rag-
woven rugs that carry the farmhouse
stamp of approval. Natural rugs and
mats made of materials such as jute and
sisal as well as woven cedar bark and
plaited rush, add subtle color and texture. Some of these natural straw mats
are sold to be used at the house entrance

Labels on canisters: Oil · Vinegar · Oatmeal · Ginger · Tea · Nutmeg · Coffee · Allspice · Sugar · Cloves · Rice · Pep

for removing dirt from shoes but would be serviceable as well as attractive used indoors.

Windows

Many farmhouse windows are best left unadorned, especially if they frame a beautiful view. If black windows at night bother you or if you have an unsightly view, opt for simple window treatments. Curtain rods as well as support brackets can be crafted from branches. Use the natural Y-shaped fork for the brackets. Use wooden shutters, bamboo shades, or wooden venetian blinds to add texture and warmth.

Details

Wainscoting

Nothing says farmhouse—rustic farmhouse—more than wainscot, whether left natural, painted green, or washed with a subtle coat of white. Keep an eye out for scraps of wainscoting at tag sales or salvage yards.

Fabrics

Learn to recycle by creating new uses for old material. Be on the lookout for doilies, fancy hand towels, and crocheted dresser scarves to use as window

Cheerful beaded flowers help brighten this twig swag that trims a kitchen window.

88

For quick-and-easy displays, frame pressed flowers, herbs, and leaves.

valances. Buy vintage textiles such as blankets, quilts, or remnant feed sacks to turn into pillows, throws, tablecloths, or seat covers. Frame snippets of homespun fabrics for charming wall art.

Note: Fabric is best framed under Plexiglas™ because it keeps out harmful sunlight.

Accessories

Walls

Glue twigs and bark on old frames and add mirrors to create a natural surrounding while adding a feeling of space and light to a room. For quick-and-easy displays, frame pressed flowers, herbs, and leaves.

Improvise—pictures of pinecones, ferns, seeds, and pods are precious pieces of natural artwork.

Think decorative—use china plates from your grandmother or someone else; show off a collection of miniature twig chairs or straw hats.

Think practical—make wall sconces with folded-bark shades; baskets for storage and serving; twig hat racks, pegs, hooks, and shelves for storage, plants, and books.

Set the stage for autumn entertaining with this eclectic display of country treasures, including brown Transferware and wood-handled flatware. Each place setting sports a Lilliputian twig chair, as well as ribbon-tied checked dish towels for napkins.

Gather acorns, pinecones, moss, twigs, and pieces of bark to add color and texture to your room setting.

Furniture

Look for built-in cupboards at buildings slated for demolition. These are often found at giveaway prices and can be reborn by adding backs to them and using them as freestanding pieces.

Tables and Tabletops

Put nature's bounty in a starring role—bowls or baskets heaped with apples, pears, squashes, and nuts are a farmhouse staple arrangement. Gather acorns, pinecones, moss, twigs, and pieces of bark to add color and texture to your room setting. Fill large crocks or tin pails with bouquets of bare branches and fern fronds for a farmhouse masterpiece. Include the unexpected; turn off the lights and illuminate your rooms with candles or oil lamps for a special party.

The light from this raffia shade casts a soft glow on the rustic bamboo tabletop decoupaged with pages torn from books. A horse-head printed pillow and plaid camp blanket add whimsy to the elegant blue-velvet platform rocker.

painted imitation birch bark

Materials

Artist's acrylic paints in white, black, and green
Paintbrush
Natural sea sponge
Stiff piece of cardboard or card stock

Step One

Paint the background of the cardboard white.

Step Two

Mix in a small amount of white and black to make light gray.

Step Three

Rinse the sponge in water and wring it out until it is almost dry. Dip the damp sponge into the gray paint, then dapple the gray over the white base coat in a few spots. Repeat with the green, using a light pecking motion to produce a soft look.

Step Four

Pour a small amount of black paint onto a paper plate and dip the edge of the cardboard in the paint. Using a quick, steady hand, press the cardboard edge down on the surface, creating thin lines.

Tip: Use paint sparingly; don't overload the sponge. To achieve the subtle, natural appearance of birch bark, vary the intensity of the colors and the black lines. To soften the work, dab a wash over the piece after the paint has dried. To protect a tabletop, apply a coat of polyurethane varnish.

This sweet little table with a repaired birch leg and stretcher sports a hand-painted top resembling birch bark. Inspired by nature, this easy-to-master paint effect can transform the most humble piece of furniture into a rustic masterpiece.

This practical
method of
propping open a
farmhouse window
is an evocative
invitation to
spring.

In a corner of the den, an outstanding pair of folk-art stands team up with a country-checked sofa.

In the true rustic-country tradition of creative re-use, this unique weathervane, fashioned out of discarded license plates, shows ingenuity as well as wind direction.

Gathered from field and meadow, a country bouquet heralds the season.

What is country without a barn?
Listen and you can hear
the generations—look and you
can see their skills.

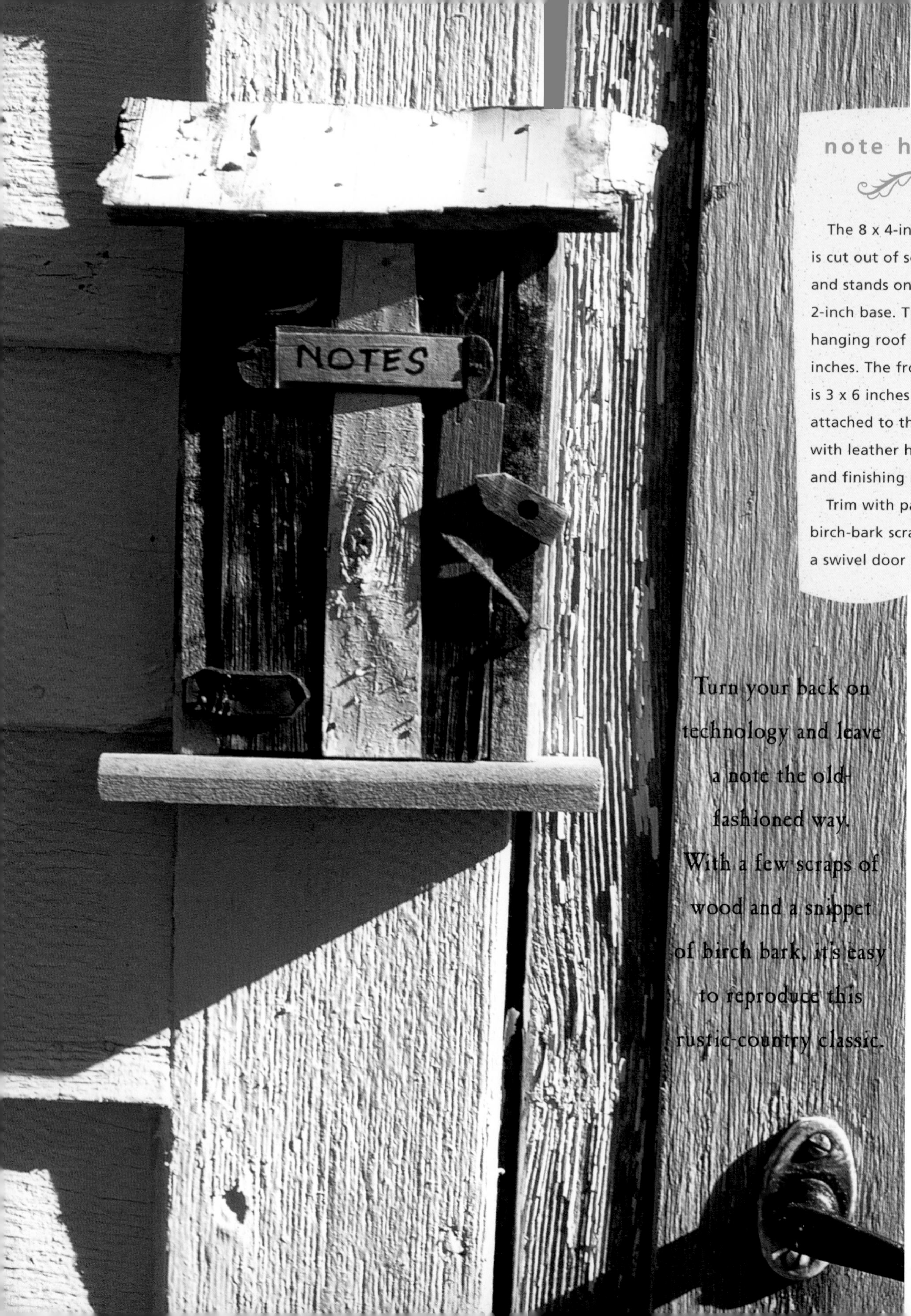

note house

The 8 x 4-inch house
is cut out of scrap wood
and stands on a 1½ x
2-inch base. The over-
hanging roof is 2 x 6
inches. The front door
is 3 x 6 inches and is
attached to the frame
with leather hinges
and finishing nails.
Trim with paper
birch-bark scraps and
a swivel door latch.

Turn your back on
technology and leave
a note the old-
fashioned way.
With a few scraps of
wood and a snippet
of birch bark, it's easy
to reproduce this
rustic country classic.

A simple hexagon birch wreath brings unexpected charm to a weathered shed.

Harmonizing hues create this country tableau resplendent with nature's tawny shades. Evidence of rustic-country charm is found in the yellow-ware bowl, overflowing with a heap of miniature baskets, as well as the twig-framed iris painting. For bookends, look no further than the woods; this pair is made from a 4-inch birch limb, cut in half.

twig coat rack

You will need a twig approximately 60 inches long and three 16-inch-long twigs for the legs, all 1 to 2 inches in diameter. Look for a straight twig with many branches and interesting shapes for the main body of the coat rack.

Note: Leg ends are tapered approximately ⅓ of the branch diameter so that they will fit flat against the coat rack.

Assemble the coat rack using pilot-hole-and-nail construction to attach legs approximately 3 inches from the bottom of the coat-rack post.

Coat racks are handy not only for wraps but for brooms and dust pans in the shop, as well as garden tools and buckets in the shed. Look for multi-forked branches like the one shown here to hurry-up your project.

pinecone finial

Drill a hole in the end of a pinecone; install a double-ended screw stud in the end of a curtain rod, and carefully screw the pinecone in place.

Tip: Since some pinecones are difficult to drill into, it is a good idea to have a selection on hand.

A natural pinecone, installed as a curtain-rod finial in this bedroom, helps define rusticity.

Well-used children's chairs often require repairs. Here a Victorian wicker rocker

had its missing arm replaced with a sanded and varnished cedar limb.

The twig antique rocker gained a woven-tape seat the colors of the flag.

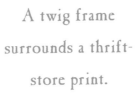

A twig frame
surrounds a thrift-
store print.

Appliquéd sheets of birch bark help breathe new life
into a table whose surface had seen better days.

An imaginative
display. A slice
of white birch—
with its ring of
bark separated—is
used to frame a
scrap of vintage
toile, much like an
embroidery hoop.

Guests are
greeted at the
front door by
a little chair.

Folks out here in
the country don't
have any set vision
of where to hang a
picture. Here a
print of a Native
American mother
and child is
displayed outside
the old toolshed.

balsam pillows

Handmade and simple, balsam bags are a favorite country item, offering the sweet scent of the forest and reminiscence of days gone by. To make your own sachets, gather balsam needles from the forest floor; using scraps of worn blankets and vintage fabrics (approximately 4 x 6 inches), stitch little pillows with facing right sides using 1/2-inch seams; leave an opening for turning. Turn and fill with balsam needles. Slip-stitch closed. When tucked into a woven bark basket, as shown here, they make an appealing addition to any setting.

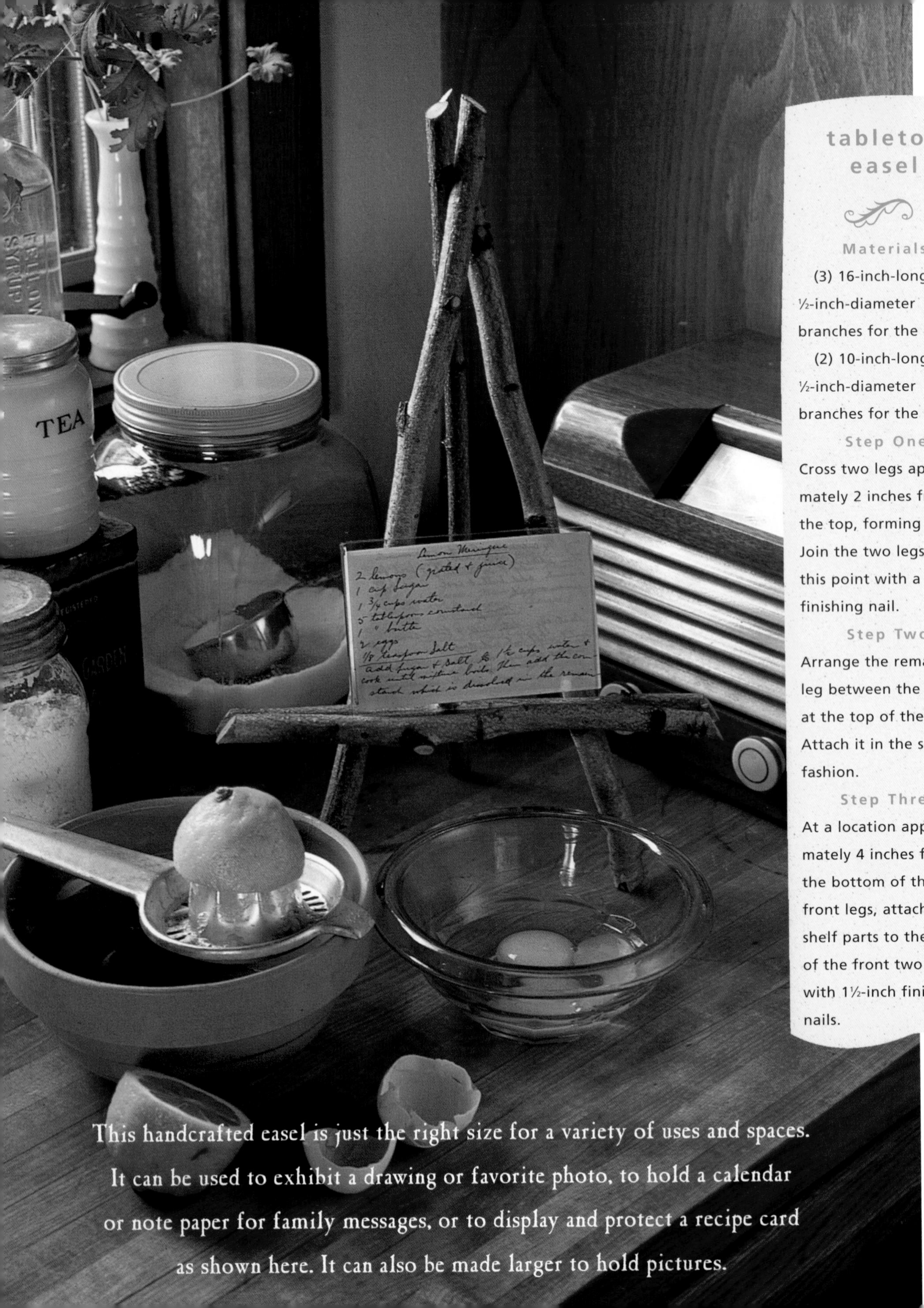

This handcrafted easel is just the right size for a variety of uses and spaces.
It can be used to exhibit a drawing or favorite photo, to hold a calendar
or note paper for family messages, or to display and protect a recipe card
as shown here. It can also be made larger to hold pictures.

Materials

Electrical lamp kit
(available at most
hardware stores)

Lightbulb and metal
shade

Hardwood branch
(approximately 72 inches
long and 1 to 2 inches
in diameter)

Note: This lamp is not
freestanding, it is
attached to the wall.
If you want to make a
freestanding floor lamp,
use the directions for
the coat rack.

Follow the instructions
on the lamp kit for
wiring the shade; use
electrical staples to
attach the wire to the
back of the branch
where it won't be seen.

A green tin shade is the origin of this charming and useful light that shines
on our rustic-revival farm table with birch panels
replacing the missing drawers. Red-and-white-checked oilcloth,
an essential farmhouse tradition, dresses up the tabletop.

A simple rustic tray makes a handy ledge
to hold an array of toiletries for the bath.

Birch bark and a vintage-rug remnant combine to transform this stepping stool into rustic-country charm.

If pansies truly tell, as the old adage goes, then this
vignette could speak volumes about the families who
lived within these farmhouse walls.

This handcrafted heirloom cradle makes a delightful storage bin for extra blankets while providing a soft spot for Miss Polly, the family doll.

Inspired by the sweet
custom of May baskets,
this ruffled Vaseline
glass epergne vase is
revamped with a wrapped
grapevine handle and filled
with pearly everlasting,
fresh from the
country meadow.

A Bennington doorknob makes a great peg for a velvet theorem, matted with peeled birch bark and edged with copper-foil tape, which can be obtained at craft stores and art-supply shops. It is intended for stained-glass work.

rustic camp and kitsch style

Capture the cabin spirit with inspiration from nature and fun-loving collectibles from the golden age of humble family summer camps.

An autumn bouquet of dried hydrangea in a classic painted willow basket sets the scene in this log-cabin home, where a blending of styles and periods evokes the simple beauty of rustic-country charm.

althought the dictionary defines *kitsch* as ". . . characterized by sentimental, often pretentious bad taste," it has come to represent objects once considered common and inferior, now propelled by nostalgia and appreciated for the warm memories they stir. Baby boomers and yuppies account for much of the interest in this memorabilia, dating mostly from their childhood or that of their grandparents. Called collectibles, these pieces generally originated in the 1930s through the early 1960s, a time when new state highways enabled families to enjoy summer retreats. While the expensive great camps of the Adirondacks displayed their rustic splendor at the turn of the century, it was only

LEFT By displaying cherished artifacts in a simple way, you are creating meaningful still lifes and writing your own rustic-country saga. Here, a pine cupboard provides the knobs for hanging a pair of inherited cowboy shirts.

RIGHT A cozy corner for little ones is tucked into the living room, creating an atmosphere that draws in the children. It's here that favorite stories of camping, fishing, butterfly hunting, and snowshoeing are told.

The key to the rustic cabin–kitsch style of decorating is mixing—but not matching—pieces.

when cars became commonplace that average families began to build cabins and cottages, called "camps," where they gathered to enjoy the simple pleasures of vacation time.

"Hit or miss" best describes camp decorating, where a mixture of rustic elements and fun furnishings makes the style. And it is with the spirit of these camps that we choose to create our own houses that say "home." The key to the rustic cabin–kitsch style of decorating is mixing—but not matching—pieces. These interiors sported wild electric hues with collections of brightly colored china and pottery. Rustic tables were often surrounded by vinyl chairs left over from 1950s classic dinette sets. Knotty-pine walls served as a gallery for "paint-by-numbers" or framed jigsaw

puzzles created on rainy afternoons at the cabin. When you think rustic cabin–kitsch, think mismatched wicker and twig chairs and loveseats, lava lamps, bread boxes, state souvenir plates, twig lamps, and birch-bark picture frames.

Given the number of garage sales and flea markets that dot the landscape on weekends nationwide, much of the appeal of adding funky finds lies in the fact that, while helping to dress a home with personality, these items are also within a lot of people's budgets.

"Leave a Note." A folded scrap of birch bark fastened with red buttons is the ideal little pocket for leaving and receiving messages when the owner of this log cabin is not at home.

Everything from the smooth polish of knotty pine to the rough texture of slab wood has been used for interior walls.

Elements of Style

Walls

It's almost impossible to think of a cozy camp along lakeside shores or on a mountain ridge without picturing the warmth of wood. Everything from the smooth polish of knotty pine to the rough texture of slab wood has been used for interior walls. Some camps sported birch-bark panels outlined with willow or alder boughs gathered from the surrounding woods. Because camps

Never mind that it's a plant stand—it is also a perfect salad server. Out here in rustic country we learn to improvise.

were often makeshift, interiors varied and many were painted. When choosing color for rustic cabin walls, deep colors taken from nature create a rugged mood. Use deep reds, earthy browns, and verdant shades of green.

Floors

While traditional camps had simple unadorned wood or stone floors, others favored patterned linoleum and painted floors. Whether you paint your floors a bright solid color or cheerfully splash and spatter paint in random dots, color-

ful floors will bring the spirit of kitsch to your abode.

Windows

Camp windows usually demanded some sort of covering in order to keep out drafts. Remnants of Pendleton and Beacon blankets make cozy curtains. Keep your eye out at thrift stores and tag sales for worn or torn blankets. Salvage the good parts and piece them together to create one-of-a-kind curtains. Heavyweight canvas shades are a no-fuss alternative.

Details

Fabrics and Linens

Vintage 1940s and 1950s table-cloths, napkins, and dish towels make wonderful additions to rustic cabins but can also stand in for pillow covers, curtains, shower curtains, lampshades, or even duvets. Prints with rustic outdoor patterns, such as camp or fishing scenes, are classic camp touches. Flower, foliage, and funky prints from the 1950s can add a desired dose of kitsch.

Accessories

Walls

Sepia-toned photographs of fishing, boating, camping, skiing, or any out-door activity make charming wall art when framed in rustic frames, as do vin-tage postcards. Art does not have to be framed; tack a map to the wall, hang a

The owner cleverly framed a collection of cigar felts under Plexiglas™ on this one-of-a-kind gun rack that doubles as a handy catchall near the front door of this log cabin.

The double-arm twig lamp provides the rustic contrast to this room setting, where a maple armchair, vintage blanket, and serape window dressing are reassuringly "camp."

Flower, foliage, and funky prints from the 1950s can add a desired dose of kitsch.

LEFT Rustic tableaux march across the room like a wallpaper border with this parade of vintage Native American prints framed in simple pine frames.

RIGHT Inspired by mountain camps, this homeowner created a rustic corner in her suburban house. North Carolina yellow poplar berry buckets hang near flea-market art and a twig-framed Native American print. To make the frame, use any good wood glue to attach the twigs to a purchased frame; when the glue dries, paint the twigs and frame forest green or a color of your choice.

flag or a hooked rug. Make copies of botanicals at the copy store and "wallpaper" a room with them using wallpaper paste. For practical storage, install floor-to-ceiling rustic twig bookshelves—colorful book jackets enhance the room and encourage reading. Hang souvenir plates, tin trays, or pennants on the walls. Any travel-related items, past or present, add bits of nostalgic charm.

Tabletops

Wooden bowls filled with river rocks, lake pebbles, or woodland moss help create a liveliness that comes from the land. Paint kitchen tables jadeite green and use heavy restaurant-style dishes and tin coffee mugs filled with Bakelite™ flatware. A wildflower bouquet presented in a vintage thermos cannot help but make a delightful and kitschy centerpiece for cabin entertaining.

Storage

Use pressed-glass jars to protect everything from sugar and flour to sewing thread and dominoes. Bark baskets are perfect for storing towels and bath oils in the bathroom. Cover recipe files with sheets of bark. Vintage lunch boxes from the 1950s and 1960s help organize family photos. Picnic tins and coolers can store myriad items for bed and bath as well as the kitchen and porch.

For practical storage, install floor-to-ceiling rustic twig bookshelves— colorful book jackets enhance the room and encourage reading.

birdhouse

Materials

Hollow log

3-pound coffee can

Step One

If you don't have a hollow log lying around, you will need a power drill to create the cavity. Make several large holes in a circular pattern, then shape the opening further with a chisel and mallet.

Step Two

Make a mark 2 inches down from the top of the log; using a drill, create a 1-inch opening through the log for an entrance hole.

Step Three

Cut three pieces of 1-inch lumber for the back, base, and roof.

Note: The back is 5½ x 13 inches; the base is 5½ x 6 inches ; the roof is 5½ x 6 inches.

Step Four

Butt the base against the back and nail the back to the base, using two or three finishing nails.

Step Five

Place the hollow log on the base with the entrance hole facing out. Attach the log to the base, at the bottom of the base, using galvanized nails.

Step Six

Join the wood roof at the back while resting the top on the log.

Step Seven

Using tin snips, cut the coffee can in half.

Step Eight

Place the can over the wooden roof and attach to the front of the roof with metal screws or finishing nails.

Tip: Cut the top of the log at a slant, making the front 1 inch shorter than the back. This permits the roof to be attached at an angle.

A winning example of rural thrift is exhibited with this hollow log birdhouse capped off with a discarded tin coffee-can roof. It is highly whimsical end products like this that reflect individual style while remaining completely functional.

Over the path and through the woods, where a ruggedly primitive shelf provides a natural ledge for a hiker's snack. Simply constructed out of a sturdy forked branch attached to a $\frac{3}{4}$-inch pine board, shelves like these can be used indoors to hold a plant or keep a stack of books tidy.

Laced with tiny
white lights, a row
of birds' nests
cavort across a
kitchen shelf along
with grapevine
branches and
assorted country
collectibles.
The nests can be
purchased at a
crafts store.

Family treasures, your own or someone else's, can produce the most welcoming still life,
such as this grouping of western elements, including a saddle, a camp blanket, a hat from a
trip to Mexico, an inherited beaded belt, a garage-sale trunk, and a rustic hat rack.

This twig wall sconce helps contribute more than light, creating a three-dimensional sculpture that complements country furnishings while remaining practical. With the addition of a cheerful polka-dot shade, it takes on an air of rustic kitsch.

When sunset settles, the glow of this twig lamp casts a subtle
light on the mellow furnishings gracing the cabin.

A collection of boxes is stacked like sculpture on this rustic mantel, organizing

favorite collectibles as well as storing sundry items.

An "as-is" rustic key holder is still serviceable, adhering to the tenets of country thrift.

A butcher-block top and stout birch legs make a sturdy coffee table for the playroom.

A vintage postcard of a Catskill Mountains cat helps set the scene. The recently acquired resin frame, simulating rustic twig work, grants a surprisingly realistic appearance when placed on natural twig bookshelves and surrounded by vintage books on nature and crafts.

Buying a bag of junk jewelry really paid off when it was turned into this marvelous lampshade—just the thing to top off the chubby white birch lamp— adding a dose of kitsch to the log cabin for a fun-loving owner.

Vintage outdoor scenes can add an authentic feel to the rustic-camp interior.

Picnic tins and
coolers can store
myriad items
for bed and bath
as well as the
kitchen.

Cedar logs, uprooted after a fierce storm, provide the needed legs for this once-discarded picnic set. With its new lease on life, it has become the setting for all seasons, with outdoor repasts served on this covered porch.

A hollow birch
log provides
shelter for nest-
building families
of wrens,
nuthatches, or
chickadees.

We look forward to meals at the cabin every year. The rustic office

hook holds bagels for breakfast and donuts at snack time.

A 9 x 10-inch piece of birch bark serves as a natural mat for a humble piece of ephemera from the owner's vast collection. Any number of images would be suitable framed in this manner, from treasured family photos and birthday greetings to happy children's drawings.

hanging mat

Materials

A print, photocopy, or photograph of your choice

Piece of birch bark of suitable size for your print

Scrap wood the same size as the bark

Wood glue

Spring-type clothespins

Twig "buttons" (slices of 3/4-inch twigs)

Tacks or nails

Chain or length of rawhide (for hanging)

Step One

Spread wood glue evenly on the back of the bark and the front of the scrap wood; press the two pieces together. Secure with clothespins along the outside edges. Allow to dry overnight.

Step Two

Position the print in the center of the bark. Nail the buttons in place through the bark and wood backing only, being careful not to nail into the print.

Note: the buttons overlap the print.

Step Three

Attach a chain, as pictured, for hanging.

Ready to cultivate
the quiet pleasures
of winter, a pair of
snowshoes awaits
service along the
trail on the way
to the lake.

IN THE GOOD OLD SUMMER-TIME

CAMPING IN THE ADIRONDACKS, N. Y.

welcome sign

Greet guests with a welcome spelled out in twigs.

Use straight twigs and finishing nails to nail the letters to a weathered board.

Tip: Create playful signs by bending small pliable branches into letters, taking advantage of their natural forks and shapes.

A universal one-word greeting formed of twigs inspires dreams of simple pleasures where that favorite place is "home-sweet-home" and friends are always welcome.

willow and bark frame

Materials

Selection of branches, ranging in length from 5 to 21 inches and ¾-inch in diameter

Assortment of bark sheets, at least 6 x 9 inches

Galvanized flathead nails (#2p and #4p)

Hammer

10 x 10-inch painting or print

Step One

Cut branches in the following sizes: two branches, 14 inches long; two branches, 17 inches long, two branches, 21 inches long; two branches, 23 inches long; 4 branches, 5 inches long.

Step Two

Follow the photo to assemble the frame.

Step Three

Arrange bark sheets on the back of the construction, and, using a staple gun or tacks, attach the bark to the frame sections.

Step Four

Add painting or print from the back, securing it with a staple gun or tacks.

This eye-catching picture frame can be crafted in an afternoon. Add a mirror for a simple yet elegant look, or use a garage-sale primitive such as this deer with purple sky for a kitschy piece of wall art.

151

Picnics on the lake are drawing to a close, and we'll need a few blankets now in case the wind starts up.

key caddie

Materials

Slab wood

Wood glue

Birch bark

Shaker pegs

Step One

Obtain a piece of slab wood from either a lumber mill or a craft store.

Step Two

Using wood glue, attach a piece of birch bark on the front of the slab wood. When the glue dries, nail the Shaker pegs in place and attach a flexible piece of willow for a hanger on the back with finishing nails.

Keep track of the keys to the cabin with this easy-to-make pegged holder, which adds a rustic look to any room.

floor lamp

Materials

For the body of the lamp you will need one birch pole, 36 to 39 inches in length and 3 inches in diameter, and a 17-inch-tall discarded organ-stool base.

A 1¼-inch-diameter, 10-inch-long dowel is required for joining the log to the stool base. If you are unable to locate an organ stool, keep your eye out for a suitable base such as fragments of old porch railings, horn footstools, wooden buckets, or pedestal table legs cut down to size. If all else fails, three 2-inch-diameter birch logs 17 inches long can be added as shown on the twig coat rack (see page 103). You will also need a lamp kit (available in most hardware stores and home centers), a light bulb, and an attractive lampshade.

A note about lampshades. A lampshade can make the lamp. Old lampshades are frequently great bargains at flea markets, and once a wire frame is free of its torn and tattered covering, it can be recovered in any number of materials, such as rag, vine, or raffia weaving; lace or vintage ticking slipcovers; or wired-on buttons. Use your imagination to create a personal shade. Don't let stains be a deterrent on paper shades; if the size of the shade is right for the base, old postcards, scraps of wallpaper, or even torn newspaper can be glued on. Look at shades with an open mind; use a glue gun to attach a bouquet of silk flowers or a bevy of pinecones.

Tools

A single-bit axe is used for cutting the tree, and a crosscut handsaw and garden clippers are needed for trimming protruding thin branches. A drill with a selection of bits (including one 12-inch-long drill bit and a spade bit) is required. Keep a ruler and pencil handy for measuring and marking. You will also need safety goggles and heavy work gloves.

Step One

Using the drill and a ⅜-inch bit 12 inches long, drill at a slant through the top of the log and out the back.

Note: The base of an organ stool has an opening approximately 1¼ inches in diameter that previously accommodated the seat.

Step Two

In order to join the pole to the base, you must drill through the bottom of the birch pole to a depth of approximately 8 inches, using the spade bit.

Step Three

Install the 10-inch dowel in the base.

Note: This is the plug that joins the two elements.

Step Four

Connect the base to the pole by inserting the dowel in the base. Use a sharp knife to trim the dowel and ensure a tight fit.

Step Five

Add the electrical parts according to the directions of the purchased kit.

A white birch limb married to a polished walnut organ stool base forms this floor lamp,
fit for an Adirondack great camp. The vintage-silk drum shade is brought up-to-date with
the addition of the wood tassel trim, reminding us of heavy Victorian fringe.

Little details can make a big impact. Consider the many uses for a simple forked branch. Here, wrapped in bailing wire, it serves as a holder for locks and keys. These natural hooks stand ready to hold a variety of personal paraphernalia, from kitchen utensils and napkin rings to belts and hair ribbons, as well as drying herbs.

resources

Antiques Shops

Cottage and Camp Antiques
99 Tinker Street
Woodstock, NY 12498
914-679-6499

Last Chance Cheese and Antiques
Main Street
Tannersville, NY 12485
518-589-6424

Lake Placid Antiques Center
105 Main Street
Lake Placid, NY 12946
518-523-3913

Laura Fisher Antiques
1050 Second Avenue
Gallery #84
New York, NY 10022
212-838-2596

Mary Kay Darrah
33 Ferry Street
New Hope, PA 18938
215-862-5927

Stone House Gallery
Natalia Pohrebinska
102 Partion Street
Saugerties, NY 12477
914-247-0827

www.tias.com
A locator of antiques shops and dealers worldwide, sorted by state, with maps.

Galleries, Shops, and Contemporary Rustic Artisans

Added Oomph!
P.O. Box 6135
High Point, NC 27262
919-869-6379

Adirondack Store and Gallery
109 Saranac Avenue
Lake Placid, NY 12946
518-523-2646
Also at:
90 Main Street
New Canaan, CT 06840
203-972-0221

Camps and Cottages
2109 Virginia Street
Berkeley, CA 94709-1613
510-548-2267

Fabulous Treecraft Furniture
Steve Heller
Route 28
Boiceville, NY 12412
914-657-6317

The Gilded Carriage
95 Tinker Street
Woodstock, NY 12498
914-679-2607

La Lune Collection
930 East Burleigh
Milwaukee, WI 53212
414-263-5300

Judd Weisberg
Route 42
Lexington, NY 12452
518-989-6583

Home Accessories and Rustic Materials

Adirondack Rustic Designs
800-411-8966
www.adkdesign.com
Rustic furnishings.

Good Wood Ltd.
Route 2 Box 447A
Bethel, VT 05032
802-234-5534

Intermares Trading
Company
Box 617
Lindenhurst, NY 11757
800-229-2263
Bamboo and cane.

Jerry Farrell
P.O. Box 255
Sidney Center, NY 13839
607-369-4916
Birch bark and birch
poles.

Loose Ends
503-390-7457
www.looseends.com
Twig pencils, birch bark,
and other accessories.

Old Hickory Furniture
Company, Inc.
Shelbyville, IN 46176
800-232-BARK
www.hickorychair.com

Fabric

Waverly Fabrics
212-213-7900
ext. 7753 or 7921
"Garden Seats" Cabin
Fever Collection #7220.

Country House Fabrics
3251 Corte Malpaso,
  Ste. 504
Camarillo, CA 93012
805-482-2006
www.countryhousefab-
rics.com

Wallpaper

Mountain Style by
Seabrook
Wide range of cabin-wall
and birch-bark wallpaper
can be purchased through
either of the following
companies.

National Decorating
800-260-1987
www.nationaldecorating.
com

American Blind and
Wallpaper Factory
800-575-8016
www.abwf.com

Museums

Adirondack Museum
P.O. Box 99
Blue Mountain Lake, NY
12812
518-353-7311

Buffalo Bill Museum
720 Sheridan Avenue
Cody, WY 82414
307-271-1620

Shelburne Museum
P.O. Box 10
Route 7
Shelburne, VT 05482
802-985-3344

Magazines

Adirondack Life
P.O. Box 97
Jay, NY 12941-0097

Country Home
1716 Locust Street
Des Moines, IA
  50309-3023

Country Living
224 W. 57th Street
New York, NY 10019
www.countryliving.com

Country Sampler's
WEST
Sampler Publications

707 Kautz Road
St. Charles, IL 60174
708-377-8000

Farm and
Ranch Living
5400 S. 60th Street
Greendale, WI 53129

Harrowsmith
Country Life
Ferry Road
Charlotte, VT 05445

Log Home
164 Middle Creek Road
Cosby, TN 37722
800-345-5647

Log Home Living
703-222-9411
www.loghomeliving.com

Catalogs (Mail Order)

Eddie Bauer Home
P.O. Box 182639
Columbus, OH 43218
800-426-8020

Gurney's Seed and
Nursery Company
110 Capital Street
Yankton, SD 57079
605-665-1930
605-665-9718 fax

North Style
Northwoods Trail
P.O. Box 6529
Chelmsford, MA
  01824-0929
800-336-5666

Mostly clothing, but a few great rustic surprises.

Pendleton Home
8550 SE McLoughlin
    Blvd.
Portland, OR 97222-6395
877-796-4663
Pendleton blankets and
rustic furnishings.

Plow & Hearth
P.O. Box 5000
Madison, VA 22727-1500
800-627-1712

Real Goods
200 Clara Avenue
Ukiah, CA 95482-4004
800-762-7325

Sheperd's Garden Seeds
30 Irene Street
Torrington, CT
    06790-6658
860-482-3638
860-482-0532 fax

Sundance
3865 West 2400 South
Salt Lake City, UT 84120
800-422-2770

The Vermont
Country Store
P.O. Box 3000
Manchester Center, VT
    05255-3000
802-362-8440
802-362-0285 fax

Whispering Pines
43 Ruane Street
Fairfield, CT 06430
800-836-4662

Books—
Vintage and
Contemporary

Beard, D. C. *New Ideas
for American Boys, The
Jack of All Trades.* New
York: Charles Scribner's
Sons, 1910.

———. *Shelters, Shacks,
and Shanties.* New York:
Charles Scribner's Sons,
1914.

Blackburn, Graham. *The
Illustrated Encyclopedia
of Woodworking:
Handtools, Instruments &
Devices.* New York:
Simon and Schuster, 1974.

Cobleigh, Rolfe. *Handy
Farm Devices and How to
Make Them.* New York:
Orange Judd and
Company, 1914.

Fields, Curtis P. *The
Forgotten Art of Building
a Stone Wall.* Dublin, NH:
Yankee, Inc., 1971.

Gilborn, Alice and Craig.
*Museum of the
Adirondacks.* Blue
Mountain Lake: The
Adirondack Museum of
the Adirondack Historical
Association, 1984.

Gilborn, Craig.
*Adirondack Furniture and
the Rustic Tradition.* New
York: Harry N. Abrams,
Inc., 1987.

Kephart, Horace. *Camping and Woodcraft*, 2 vols. New York: Macmillan, 1918.

Kylloe, Ralph. *Cabin Collectibles*. Salt Lake City: Gibbs Smith, Publisher, 2000.

———. *Rustic Artistry for the Home*. Salt Lake City: Gibbs Smith, Publisher, 2000.

———. *Rustic Traditions*. Salt Lake City: Gibbs Smith, Publisher, 1993.

Mack, Daniel. *Log Cabin Living*. Salt Lake City: Gibbs Smith, Publisher, 1999.

———. *Making Rustic Furniture*. New York: Sterling/Lark, 1992.

Murray, Reverend William Henry Harrison. *Adventures in the Wilderness or Camp Life in the Adirondacks*. Boston: Fields, Osgood, and Company, 1869.

Nearing, Helen and Scott. *Living the Good Life: How to Live Sanely and Simply in a Troubled World*. New York: Schocken Books, 1970.

———. *The Maple Sugar Book*. New York: Schocken Books, 1950.

Ruoff, Abby. *Making Rustic Originals*. Point Roberts, WA/Vancouver, BC: Hartley and Marks Publishers, Inc., 1999.

———. *Making Twig Furniture and Household Things*. Point Roberts, WA/Vancouver, BC: Hartley and Marks Publishers, Inc., 1991, 1995.

———. *Making Twig Garden Furniture*. Point Roberts, WA/Vancouver, BC: Hartley and Marks Publishers, Inc., 1997.

Schaffiner, Cynthia V. A. *Discovering American Folk Art*. New York: Harry N. Abrams, Inc., 1991.

Seton, Ernest Thompson. *The Library of Pioneering and Woodcraft*. Garden City, NY: Doubleday Page and Co., 1927.

Sloane, Eric. *Diary of an Early American Boy*. New York: Ballantine, 1965.

———. *A Museum of Early American Tools*. New York: Ballantine, 1964.

Smyser, Carol A. *Nature's Design: A Practical Guide to Natural Landscaping*. Emmaus, PA: Rodale Press, 1982.

Wicks, William S. *Log Cabins: How to Build and Furnish Them*. New York: Forest and Stream Publishing Company, 1889.

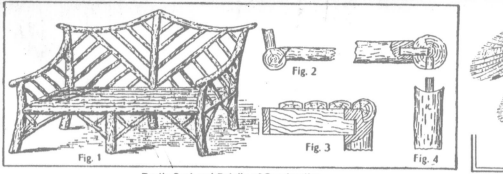

Rustic Seat and Details of Construction

How to Make a Rustic Seat

The rustic settee illustrated in Fig. 1 may be made 6 ft. long, which will accommodate four average-sized persons. It is not advisable to exceed this length, as then it would look out of proportion, says the Wood-Worker. Select the material for the posts, and for preference branches that are slightly curved, as shown in the sketch. The front posts are about 3½ in. in diameter by 2 ft. 4 in. long. The back posts are 3 ft. 4 in. high, while the center post is 3 ft. 8 in. in height. The longitudinal and transverse rails are about 3 in. in diameter and their ends are pared away to fit the post to which they are connected by 1-in. diameter dowels. This method is shown in Fig. 4. The dowel holes are bored at a distance of 1 ft. 2½ in. up from the lower ends of posts. The front center leg is partially halved

rails, and are then secured with two or three brads at each end.

Select curved pieces, about 2½ in. in diameter, for the arm rests and back rails; while the diagonally placed filling may be about 2 in. in diameter. Start with the shortest lengths, cutting them longer than required, as the paring necessary to fit them to the rails and posts shortens them a little. Brad them in position as they are fitted, and try to arrange them at regular intervals.

WREN HOUSE

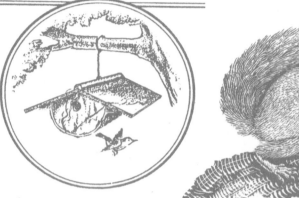

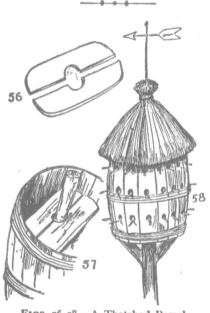

FIGS. 56-58.—A Thatched Barrel.

A Barrel for a Martin-House

which, when neatly made and thatched with straw, is decidedly ornamental, and will be duly appreciated by your bird friends.

If we can keep the English sparrows away, the bluebirds will nest in any sort of a sheltered hole.

Earthenware flower-pots, as shown in Fig. 59, may be used for bird-houses if you

A FERN BASKET

xpenditure of five cents, and with tle trouble, any intelligent boy can tty fern basket. Let us go out ods and collect some oak branches e-quarters of an inch thick, and length from six inches to twelve

round the hole, putting the two right sides of the material together. When this is done, and

A FERN BASKET FOR

FOR an expenditure of five cents, and with very little trouble, any intelligent boy can make a pretty fern basket. Let us go out into the woods and collect some oak branches about three-quarters of an inch thick, and varying in length from six inches to twelve inches. We shall require between thirty and forty pieces altogether for our purpose.

When we take these home, we must score down the bark from end to end of the sticks, and then, having put them in a pail, we pour boiling water on them. The effect of the scalding will be to strip off the bark, leaving us nothing but the bare sticks, which are just what we want for our purpose.

Besides the sticks which we have collected, all the material we require is a little copper or brass wire, which we can purchase for five cents. Copper or brass wire is better than iron wire, because iron wire would rust through and waste away. It will be seen that the basket tapers from about twelve inches square at the top to about six inches square at the bottom. Of course, we need not keep to these sizes; we can make the basket four inches at the bottom and eight inches at the top, or any other size that we find convenient.

We may colour the sticks by putting them into water in which we have put a small amount of permanganate of potash or of logwood.

the French or ribbon

The forme the latter We requir oak sticks to split th must be s if we cann the sticks

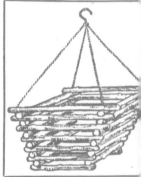

THE BASKET READY FOR U

and gravel with good When we w to pour should tak in water, Rain or will do if

5665